50 REASONS MY TODDLER IS CRYING

An illustrated tale
of assorted world-ending meltdowns

Angela Foy Davis

50 REASONS MY TODDLER IS CRYING
All Rights Reserved
Copyright © 2020, Angela Foy Davis

Written and drawn by Angela Foy Davis

ISBN: 978-0-578-67499-5

Printed in the United States of America

To all the parents of little ones out there...
I promise the madness is worth it!

♥

1. I wouldn't let him take the foot tambourine into bed with him.

2. He wanted some cheese.

3. I gave him some cheese.

4. I wouldn't let him climb into the oven.
(It was on.)

5. He couldn't find Jadon.

6. He found Jadon.

7. We wouldn't let him stick a chopstick into his eye.

unpoked Eyes →

8. These toys were not lined up perfectly straight.

9. He REALLY wanted to take off his pants.

10. He has no pants.

11. Jadon was sitting on the couch.

12. I wouldn't open the birdhouse for
     him. (It doesn't open.)

13. A CRUMB WAS STUCK TO THE BOTTOM OF HIS FOOT.

14. He wanted to build a marble run, so I built him a marble run.

15. Marbles were going down the holes.

16. The marble run got rage-destroyed by some mysterious unnamed force of fury, and now there is no more marble run.

17. There were kids playing on the public playground. #TheAudacity

18. His sleeves were rolled up.

19. THERE ARE BALLS IN THE BALL PIT.
#PitOfDespair

20. *We were at a wedding.*

21. They weren't playing the song he was asking for. (The bride was actively walking down the aisle.)

22. I wouldn't let him take the candle from the wedding favors table.

23. The table fell over on him.

24. I wouldn't let him pour an entire bottle of water onto the floor at cocktail hour.

25. We had to leave the wedding.

(In all seriousness, it was BEAUTIFUL
and I'm so thankful we were able to
be there!)

#MemoriesForaLifetime
#LoveMyPatientFamily
#ThisIsWhyWeDontGoToStuff

26. He wanted some of my rice. I gave him some rice.

27. There's food all over his plate.
#ItsAHardknockLife

28. Daddy was in the way of his tantrum.

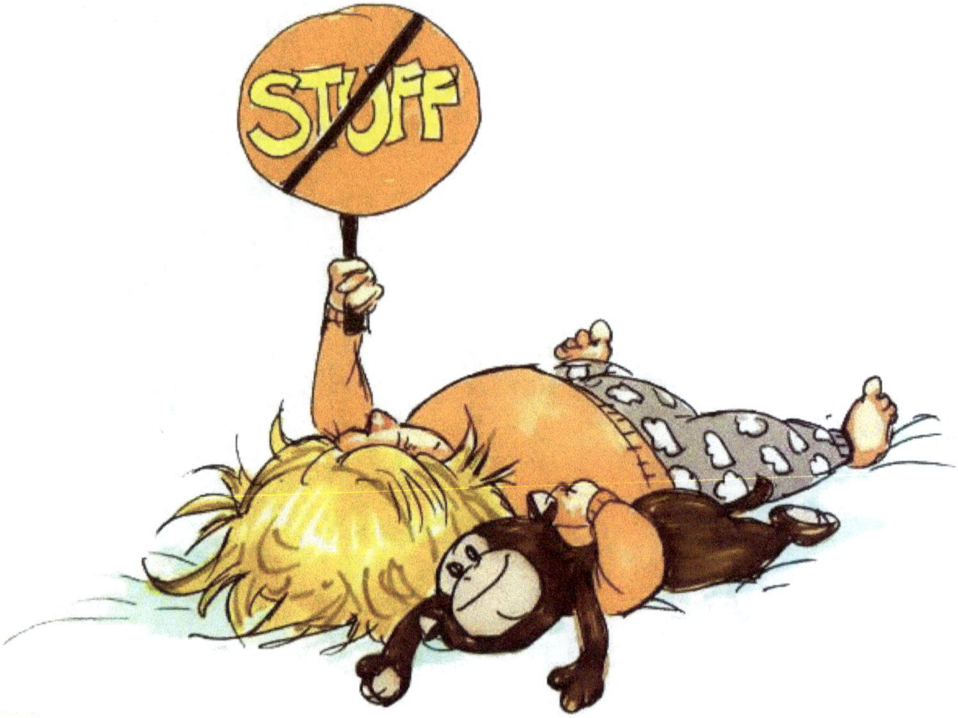
STUFF

29. He woke up.

30. I put pants on him.

In fairness, he'd been wearing shorts all summer, and he wasn't used to the horrific feel of fabric covering his legs... Who among us can't relate?

As soon as I removed the offending pants, he was instantly fine.

AND THEN...

31. There was a cup of water sitting on the table.

32. Jadon was sitting at the table.

33. A noodle fell on the floor.

34. **A FLAX SEED FELL ON THE FLOOR.**

#GonnaBeALongWeekend

#PleasePrayForUs

35. At Target, I wouldn't let him remove the cardboard things from all the shoes and take them home with us.

36. The cabinet door was open a millimeter and won't close completely.

37. My hair was in a ponytail.

38. He threw a toy at Jadon and Jadon started crying.

39. The marble was blue.

40. I said the word "turtle."

41. He wanted some banana. NO, not that piece he's holding. NAY, GOOD SIR. A different and apparently vastly superior piece of banana.

He's so mad he's pulling his pants off.

#ParentsJustDontUnderstand

42. We wouldn't let him lovingly body-slam the cats.

43. He wanted to take a cushion off the couch.

44. He wanted ALL the cushions removed.

45. He wanted to stand all the cushions up..."like dominos." (Heaven help us)

46. Cushions did NOT stand up like dominos.

#StupidGravity
#GrandAmbitions

47. We wouldn't give him any
"maybelater." *

*He asked for some chocolate cake, to which Daddy replied, "We're not having cake right now, buddy. We'll have some maybe later."

So he asked for some "maybelater." Logically.

48. The sun was bright, and he wanted me to turn it off. I could not.

49. He wanted me to sing, and I asked him what song.

50. He wouldn't choose, so I chose a song at random.

I chose...poorly.

Honorable Mention Meltdowns:

• Some fool said "good morning" to him.

• I handed him the wrong duckie during bath. (They're all identical.)

• I washed his hair. (I can't even express the horror of this occurrence.)

• He asked for some "veggies," and was given some veggies. (Hint: What he actually wanted was apparently NOT veggies.)

• He noticed that the LEGO he had set on his dresser before nap had been moved an inch.

He noticed this. <u>In the dark</u>.

Whatever you're going through today,
I hope this little book gives you a smile.
And if you have your own crazy munchkins,
take heart:

You aren't alone!

The crazy will come and go, sanity will
return, and the sun will rise each day.

And I still won't be able to turn it off when Kai asks me to.

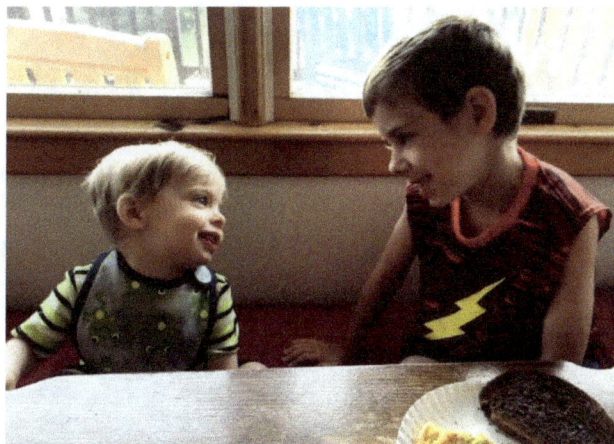

(See? He isn't always crying!)

Angela Foy Davis lives in Virginia with her awesome husband, their two amazing boys, Jadon and Kai, and their two cats, Cait and Renji (who have thus far survived Kai's affections).

♥

www.ingramcontent.com/pod-product-compliance
Lightning Source LLC
LaVergne TN
LVHW081337060426
835513LV00014B/1323